ANIMAL PREDATORS

Eagles

SANDRA MARKLE

⌐ LERNER PUBLICATIONS COMPANY / MINNEAPOLIS

THE ANIMAL WORLD IS FULL OF
PREDATORS.

Predators are the hunters that find, catch, and eat other animals—their prey—in order to survive. Every environment has its chain of hunters. The smaller, slower, less able predators become prey for the bigger, faster, more cunning hunters. And everywhere, there are just a few kinds of predators at the top of the food chain. *In wilderness areas on every continent, this group of predators includes one or more kinds of eagles, like this golden eagle.*

Why are eagles such great hunters? For one thing, eagles, like this Philippine eagle, can swoop through the air at a great speed and strike with strong, sharp claws called talons. Most eagles hunt during the day. Their large eyes have powerful magnifying lenses and lots of cells that pick up light. Together, they help eagles see long distances in great detail. Eagles can see small prey on the ground while soaring high overhead. Because their eyes face forward, eagles can judge the distance between themselves and their prey.

For protection and support, an eagle's eyes are surrounded by bony tubes in its head. These tubes limit how much an eagle's eyes can move. To look left, right, up, or down, an eagle—like this young harpy—must turn its head. An eagle's head can move easily, though. In fact, it can turn its head far enough to look almost straight behind itself.

Whatever direction the eagle is looking, it is most often on the lookout for prey. This female golden eagle is hunting from her perch on a craggy Colorado mountain. Her tawny brown feathers blend in with her rock perch. This helps her go unnoticed while she watches the prairie below for moving prey.

When she spies a prairie dog feeding alone, the golden eagle launches into flight. Her outstretched wings stretch nearly 7 feet (2 meters) from tip to tip. Golden eagles are one of the world's largest eagles. The female, weighing about 15 pounds (7 kilograms), is nearly one-third bigger than her mate. Female eagles need to be larger so they can catch larger prey when they get the chance. That way females don't have to spend as much energy hunting to get the food they need. They will need this extra energy to produce their eggs.

With a couple of powerful wing flaps, the female eagle heads in pursuit of her prey. Her skeleton, made up mostly of light, hollow bones, helps her flight. Her body is covered by more than seven thousand feathers to keep her warm. All the eagle's feathers together weigh no more than 21 ounces (586 grams)—less than two cans of soda. They do their job without adding extra weight to slow the eagle down.

Her feathers work to help her slip easily through the air. Tiny hooks on the feathers zip them together and streamline her body. The feathers are thicker on the top of her wings than underneath. Air slides quickly over the tops of the wings. The air flows more slowly under her wings. This creates a lift that holds her up. The primaries, the long feathers at the tips of her wings, can flex and not break as they sweep through the air. These feathers spread apart like fingers so the air flows through easily.

Each downward stroke of the eagle's wings, powered by her large breast muscles, moves her forward as she homes in on her prey.

When she's nearly over the prairie dog, the female golden eagle folds her wings and dives. She plunges through the air, reaching a speed of nearly 190 miles (300 kilometers) per hour. Just before she reaches her prey, she pops open her wings. The open wings act as brakes, slowing her down as she thrusts out her talon-tipped feet to attack.

Just in the nick of time, the prairie dog ducks into an entrance to its colony's underground tunnels. Having missed her target, the golden eagle pumps her wings and sweeps upward again. The prairie dog pokes its head out and yips an alarm cry. Other prairie dogs yip too, spreading the warning that a predator is nearby.

Hearing this call and seeing prairie dogs scurrying for shelter, the eagle moves on. She rides a rising current of warm air higher and higher. High above the earth, the eagle spreads her big wings. She glides on the air currents, saving energy while she continues to search for prey.

The eagle spots a rabbit and swoops down. Wings and tail adjust her angle of attack as her feet thrust forward. *Bam!* Her fast-moving body slams her talons into the rabbit's body. Her toes—three facing forward and one backward—clamp down. Strong leg muscles power the grip of the eagle's claws. These muscles, attached to the bird's feet by stretchy tendons, pull her toes together. They drive the talons into the rabbit. The kill happens so quickly that the rabbit has no time to struggle and damage the eagle's wings.

The golden eagle settles on the ground and folds her wings. She uses her sharp-edged, hooked beak to slice through the prey's skin and tear meat off its bones. An eagle's beak is hard bone covered with a thin layer of keratin. Keratin is similar to the material that makes up human fingernails. She has no teeth to chew with. Instead, she gulps down the chunks of meat.

Once she's eaten some of the meat, the prey is light enough for her to carry. The female golden eagle heads home to her nest with the remains of her prey held tightly in her talons.

At the nest, her mate and their two chicks wait for her. The chicks are less than two weeks old. They have only a thin covering of downy feathers, not enough to keep them warm. The parents take turns staying on the nest while the other hunts. That way, the chicks will always have one parent to huddle against to stay warm. The parent on the nest also guards against flying predators, such as hawks, that might try to attack and eat the chicks.

When the female lands, she drops her prey. As she walks across the nest, she balls her feet into tight fists and then spreads them out again to stand. Both parents do this when they move around the nest so they don't injure the chicks with their sharp talons.

The male leaves to hunt, and the chicks beg to be fed. The female rips a piece of meat off the prey's bones with her beak. She dangles the piece until a chick grabs it. She continues to offer the pieces this way until the meat is gone or the chicks have eaten their fill.

By tearing off strips of meat, the female avoids feeding the chicks any bits, like fur or bone, that could be difficult for the chicks to digest. But like all adult eagles, she gulps down chunks of food—fur, bone, and all. The chunks pass into her stomach and then into a muscular sac called the gizzard. The gizzard grinds up the food before it passes into the intestines to complete digestion. The hard waste bits stay in the gizzard, and a few hours after eating, the female golden eagle throws up a pellet of those wastes.

For more than a month, the male and female golden eagles take turns hunting prey to feed themselves and their chicks. But once the eaglets are about five weeks old, they need more food than one hunting parent can provide. Then both parents must devote most of their time to hunting food for their young.

Fortunately, the chicks are old enough to be left alone on the nest. They are bigger and have begun to grow their adult feathers. Their beaks and talons are strong enough to defend themselves. They are also able to feed themselves, tearing up the prey their parents bring home.

A pair of golden eagles needs to catch a lot of prey to raise their young successfully. To do this, they adopt a home range. This is an area where they live and hunt. Having a home range means they get to know the area well and learn where they are likely to find prey. This way, they don't have to use as much energy searching for a meal.

The male golden eagle sets out to hunt across his home range. He soon sights another male golden eagle drifting through the air below him. He folds his wings and plunges toward the outsider to drive him away. When the rival still doesn't leave, the male attacks. Their screams sound like chunks of broken glass scratching together. The pair flaps their wings hard and strike at each other with their sharp talons. Finally, the intruder breaks free and flies away.

Another reason eagles are successful predators is that their chicks get plenty of care and training from their parents. Harpy eagles, which live in the forests of Central and South America, need about ten months of care. The adults must devote all their hunting efforts to raising a single young. That's why, although the female lays two eggs, she stops sitting on them as soon as one chick hatches. The harpy eagles won't have the time and strength to rear two.

Harpy eagles are armed with the biggest talons of any eagles. They are longer than an adult grizzly bear's claws. Harpy parents are able to catch and kill big prey, like this capuchin monkey, to share with their eaglets.

Well before a harpy eaglet is strong enough to start hunting, it starts to get ready for flight. While its parents hunt to bring home food, this five-month-old male harpy explores, walking along the branches around his nest. He holds on tight with his long talons to keep from falling. He often flaps his wings to exercise and strengthen them.

In North America, bald eagles hunt fish to feed themselves and their growing young. With its keen vision, a bald eagle is able to spot fish swimming beneath the surface while it soars high overhead. When a fish comes up to the surface to feed, the eagle dives and snags its prey with its talons.

Bald eagle females produce as many as three eggs, but they lay the eggs several days apart. The first chick to hatch is always a little older and bigger than its brothers or sisters. It will fight—even kill—its nest mates to get the biggest share of the food supply.

Eventually, the adult bald eagles stop bringing food back to the nest. The juveniles are now able to fly and follow the adults when they go hunting. This juvenile eagle is as big as its parent, though its feathers don't yet have adult colors. It also lacks the adult's hunting skills. The juvenile bald eagle learns by watching its parents when they hunt and by trial and error. As long as food is plentiful, the adults help their offspring by sharing their meals.

Eagles are also successful predators because they are willing to take on challenges and attack big prey. The martial eagle hunts in Africa's grasslands. It doesn't hesitate to go after prey as large as these gazelles. Swooping out of the air, it thrusts out its talons to strike a gazelle in the neck for a killing blow.

A pair of marabou storks forces this African fishing eagle into the air and away from its prey. But the eagle takes flight only to better use its talons. After several swooping attacks, the eagle drives off the storks and reclaims its prey.

By the time winter arrives with icy winds and earth-covering snows, this juvenile golden eagle is hunting alone. The eagle is still developing its skills, and many hunts end in failure. Still this youngster will survive. Eagles are willing to eat whatever they can find. So when the young adult eagle spots a carcass, it swoops down and lands to feed. True to its aggressive nature, it will drive off scavengers, like these black-billed magpies, and fight to keep its meal.

Like all eagles, the golden will become a mature hunter before it produces young. Each year the golden eagle molts, or sheds its feathers and grows new ones. This keeps its body in good flying shape. It also shows that the young eagle is maturing. In its first year, the juvenile's feathers were blackish brown. By the time the golden eagle is five years old, its feathers are golden brown. By then the golden eagle has become an expert at finding and catching prey. It is ready to mate and raise another generation of winged hunters.

Looking Back

- Look at the golden eagle flying with its prey on page 15. See how the eagle has its legs pulled up close to its body. That helps keep this added weight centered for balance. It also reduces the drag, or friction of moving through the air, as much as possible.

- Compare the golden eaglets on pages 16 and 21. In what ways have they changed as they've gotten older?

- Take another look at pages 10, 32, and 33. See how these three different kinds of eagles use the same attack strategy. They put their weapons—their talons—as far out in front of their body and vital organs as possible.

- Have a partner help you measure how far away you can stand and still see page 28 clearly. It's likely to be a lot shorter distance than the bald eagle's target range. Bald eagles are estimated to see prey clearly from as far away as about 300 feet (91 meters).

Glossary

BEAK: the hard body around the mouth. In eagles, it is hook shaped to help this hunter make its kill.

CHICK: the name given to a baby bird

EAGLET: a young eagle

FEATHER: a protective body covering unique to birds. Tiny hooks on eagle feathers zip the many strands together to provide an airtight surface.

GIZZARD: the muscular body part that helps birds break down the food they eat

JUVENILE: a young adult

MOLT: to shed and replace feathers

PELLET: compacted ball of waste—which can include bones, teeth, and fur—that the eagle throws up

PREDATOR: an animal that hunts other animals

PREY: an animal that a predator catches to eat

SCAVENGER: an animal that feeds on dead animals

STOMACH: stretchy body part that stores and begins to break down food

TALON: a claw-tipped toe

WING: body part capable of lifting the bird and moving it forward in flight

Further Information

BOOKS

Collard, Sneed. *Birds of Prey: A Look at Daytime Raptors*. Danbury, CT: Watts Library, 2000. Compare eagles to other birds of prey, such as kites and falcons.

Donovan, Sandra. *Harpy Eagles*. Chicago: Raintree, 2002. Take a tour of the Amazon rain forest while learning about the life and habits of the harpy eagle.

Savage, Candace. *The Eagles of North America*. New York: Sterling, 2000. Check out this in-depth look at the lives and traits of North America's bald eagles and golden eagles.

WEBSITES

Bird Flight

http://people.eku.edu/ritchisong/554notes2.html
Learn how birds fly. Animated graphics and video clips bring this exploration to life. Scroll down to Golden Eagle in Flight and click to observe its wing movements.

Eagle Cam Web Log

http://www.friendsofblackwater.org/eagle_cam_blog/ The links section connects to a live camera inside an eagle's nest so you can watch bald eagle young grow up

Nature: Eagles

http://www.pbs.org/wnet/nature/eagles
Read about different kinds of eagles. Learn how scientists rediscovered one kind of eagle, until recently, believed to be extinct.

Index

For Marcia Marshall who helps my ideas take flight

The author would like to thank the following people for sharing their expertise and enthusiasm: Marta Curti, Peregrine Fund's Neotropical Raptor Center, and Kent Keller, Utah Division of Wildlife Resources. The author would also like to express a special thank-you to Skip Jeffery for his help and support during the creative process.

Photo Acknowledgments

The images in this book are used with the permission of: © Yva Momatiuk & John Eastcott/Minden Pictures, p. 1; © Reuters/CORBIS, pp. 3, 5; © Neil Lucas/naturepl.com, p. 4; © Kent R. Keller, pp. 6, 7, 8, 10, 15, 16, 19, 35; © Jim Brandenburg/Minden Pictures, p. 11; © Bruno Dittrich/Stone/Getty Images, p. 13; © W. Perry Conway/CORBIS, pp. 14, 21, 37; © J. L. G. Grande/Photo Researchers, Inc., p. 18; © Laurie Campbell/NHPA/Photoshot, p. 20; © Markus Varesvuo/naturepl.com, p. 23; © Neil Rettig Productions, Inc., pp. 25, 26, 27; © Lynn M. Stone/naturepl.com, p. 28; © Louis Gagnon/naturepl.com, p. 29; © Daniel J. Cox/CORBIS, p. 31; © Jonathan and Angela/Taxi/Getty Images, p. 32; © Anup Shah/naturepl.com, p. 33.
Front Cover: © Neil McIntyre/Taxi/Getty Images.

Lerner Publications Company
A division of Lerner Publishing Group, Inc.
241 First Avenue North
Minneapolis, MN 55401 U.S.A.

Website address: www.lernerbooks.com

Websites listed in Further Reading are current at time of publication.

Library of Congress Cataloging-in-Publication Data

Markle, Sandra.
    Eagles / by Sandra Markle.
       p.   cm. — (Animal predators)
    Includes bibliographical references and index.
    ISBN 978—1—58013—519—1 (lib. bdg. : alk. paper)
    1. Eagles—Juvenile literature. I. Title.
  QL696.F32M2578 2009
  598.9'42—dc22   2008038119

Manufactured in the United States of America
1 2 3 4 5 6 — DP — 15 14 13 12 11 10